# BALTO'S STORY

by Kevin Blake

**Consultant: Harvey Webster, Director**
**Wildlife Resource Center**
**Cleveland Museum of Natural History**
**Cleveland, Ohio**

New York, New York

## Credits

Cover and Title Page, © AlphaAndOmega/Alamy, © Wikipedia/Creative Commons, © Bettmann/Corbis/AP Images, and © ventdusud/Shutterstock; TOC, © AlphaAndOmega/Alamy; 4T, © Bettmann/Corbis/AP Images; 4B, © BSIP/UIG via Getty Images; 6–7, © Carrie McLain Museum/AlaskaStock; 7, © Wikipedia/Creative Commons; 8–9, © Museum of History & Industry, Seattle; All Rights Reserved; 9T, © PF-(sdasm4)/Alamy; 10, © Randi Hausken from Bærum, Norway; 10TR, © Wolfgang Kaehler/Corbis; 11, © Alaska Stock/Alamy; 12, © Underwood & Underwood/Corbis; 13, © Wikipedia/Creative Commons; 14, © Library of Congress Prints and Photographs Division, Washington, D.C.; 15, © AP Photo; 16, © Jeff Schultz/AlaskaStock; 17, © Bettmann/Corbis/AP Images; 18, © Jean-Erick Pasquier/Gamma-Rapho; 19L, © Associated Press; 19R, © Images & Stories/Alamy; 20T, © ventdusud/Shutterstock; 20B, © chaoss/Shutterstock; 21, © Jeff Schultz/AlaskaStock; 22, © Jeff Schultz/AlaskaStock; 23, © imagebroker.net/SuperStock; 24, © Bettmann/Corbis/AP Images; 25, © Carrie McLain Museum/AlaskaStock; 26, © AlphaAndOmega/Alamy; 27T, © Al Grillo/Zumapress.com; 27B, © Michael Penn/Juneau Empire; 28, © WildLivingArts/Thinkstock; 29TL, © Eric Isselee/Shutterstock; 29TR, © Yann Arthus-Bertrand/Corbis; 29BL, © Jagodka/Shutterstock; 29BR, © Eric Isselee/Shutterstock.

Publisher: Kenn Goin
Senior Editor: Joyce Tavolacci
Creative Director: Spencer Brinker
Design: Dawn Beard Creative
Photo Researcher: Picture Perfect Professionals, LLC

*Library of Congress Cataloging-in-Publication Data*

Blake, Kevin, 1978–author.
  Balto's story / by Kevin Blake ; consultant, Harvey Webster, Director Wildlife Resource Center, Cleveland Museum of Natural History, Cleveland, Ohio.
      pages cm. — (Dog heroes)
  Includes bibliographical references and index.
  ISBN-13: 978-1-62724-286-8 (library binding)
  ISBN-10: 1-62724-286-4 (library binding)
  1. Balto (Dog)—Juvenile literature. 2. Sled dogs—Alaska—Biography—Juvenile literature.
  3. Diphtheria—Alaska—Nome—Juvenile literature. 4. Nome (Alaska)—History—Juvenile literature.
  I. Title. II. Series: Dog heroes.
  SF428.7.B53 2015
  636.73—dc23
                    2014011635

For more information, write to Bearport Publishing Company, Inc., 45 West 21st Street, Suite 3B, New York, New York 10010. Printed in the United States of America.

10 9 8 7 6 5 4 3 2 1

# Table of Contents

# A Daring Path

**Musher** Gunnar Kaasen and his **lead dog**, Balto, were battling the worst winter storm to hit Alaska in twenty years. The temperature had dropped to -50°F (-46°C). Fierce winds roared at 70 miles per hour (113 kph) as snow pounded Gunnar's sled. The blinding **blizzard** made it impossible to see.

Gunnar and Balto

At -50°F (-46°C), it's so cold that, without gloves, a person's fingers can freeze solid within minutes.

Waiting for the weather to change, however, wasn't an option. It was already February 1, 1925, and the clock was ticking fast. Fifty miles (81 km) away in Nome, Alaska, dozens of the town's children were sick and near death. Gunnar and Balto carried the only medicine that could cure them. The storm couldn't stop them. The children's lives depended on it.

Nome

Alaska

CANADA

Pacific
Ocean

UNITED STATES

Atlantic
Ocean

N
W E
S

MEXICO

Alaska is the northernmost
state in the United States.

Dogsled teams race
through a blizzard.

# Outbreak!

The emergency in Nome began nearly two weeks earlier when three-year-old Billy Barnett complained to his mother of a sore throat and fever. She took him to Dr. Curtis Welch. When he looked at Billy's throat, he feared the worst: **diphtheria**. Diphtheria is a highly **contagious** and deadly **disease** that can be cured only by a special **antitoxin**. By the time Billy saw Dr. Welch, the boy was too sick for the medicine to help him. He died later that day.

Nome, Alaska, in the 1920s

Diphtheria attacks the throat and makes it difficult for a person to breathe. Today, diphtheria has been nearly wiped out in the United States by the use of a **vaccine**.

Over the next two days, more children became sick. It was an **epidemic**! Making things worse, Dr. Welch did not have enough antitoxin to help the sick children. He begged other doctors across the country for more medicine to be sent to Nome. Without immediate help, many would die.

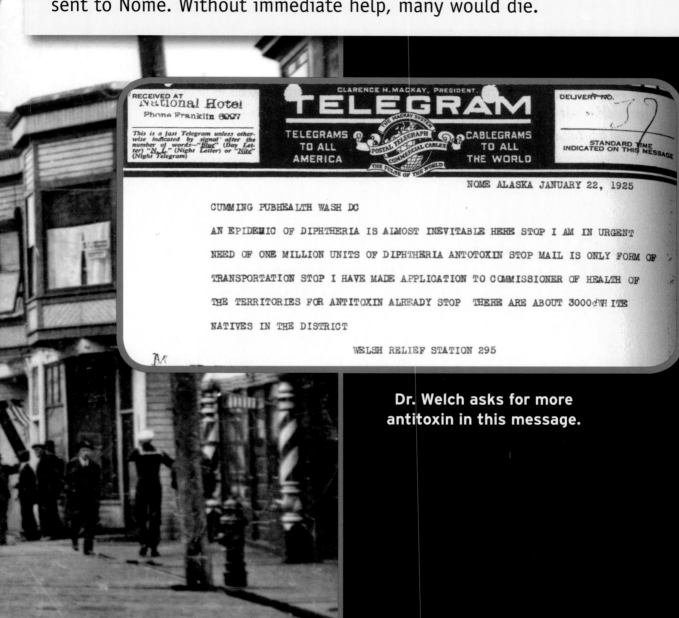

RECEIVED AT
National Hotel
Phone Franklin 6007

This is a fast Telegram unless otherwise indicated by signal after the number of words—"Blue" (Day Letter) "N.L." (Night Letter) or "Nite" (Night Telegram)

CLARENCE H. MACKAY, PRESIDENT.

**TELEGRAM**

TELEGRAMS TO ALL AMERICA

THE MACKAY SYSTEM
POSTAL TELEGRAPH
COMMERCIAL CABLES
THE PULSE OF THE WORLD

CABLEGRAMS TO ALL THE WORLD

DELIVERY NO.

STANDARD TIME INDICATED ON THIS MESSAGE

NOME ALASKA JANUARY 22, 1925

CUMMING PUBHEALTH WASH DC

AN EPIDEMIC OF DIPHTHERIA IS ALMOST INEVITABLE HERE STOP I AM IN URGENT

NEED OF ONE MILLION UNITS OF DIPHTHERIA ANTOTOXIN STOP MAIL IS ONLY FORM OF

TRANSPORTATION STOP I HAVE MADE APPLICATION TO COMMISSIONER OF HEALTH OF

THE TERRITORIES FOR ANTITOXIN ALREADY STOP  THERE ARE ABOUT 3000 WHITE

NATIVES IN THE DISTRICT

WELSH RELIEF STATION 295

**Dr. Welch asks for more antitoxin in this message.**

7

# Isolated

Doctors in Anchorage, Alaska, had antitoxin that they could share with the children of Nome. However, there was still a serious problem. Anchorage was hundreds of miles away from Nome, and there were no roads that connected the two towns. How could the medicine be transported in time to save the sick children?

Nome

ALASKA

Pacific
Ocean

Anchorage

N
W    E
S

Covering more than 600,000 square miles (1,554,000 sq km), Alaska is bigger than England, France, Spain, and Italy combined. Even today, there are still no roads connecting Nome to the rest of Alaska.

There were two options. The medicine could either be flown by airplane or carried by teams of sled dogs. The governor of Alaska thought carefully about what to do. If the plane crashed, the medicine would be lost forever. On the other hand, a flight would take only a few hours while a trip by sled dogs could take weeks.

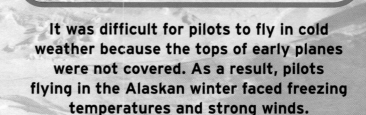

It was difficult for pilots to fly in cold weather because the tops of early planes were not covered. As a result, pilots flying in the Alaskan winter faced freezing temperatures and strong winds.

Sled dogs were used to carry mail and other important items to hard-to-reach parts of Alaska.

# Husky Power!

The governor decided to trust sled dogs for the important job. Many teams of dogs would work in a **relay**, taking turns pulling the precious medicine until it reached Nome. Siberian huskies were often used to pull sleds—and they were perfect for this challenging task. For one thing, huskies were **bred** to travel long distances in freezing weather.

Siberian huskies get ready to pull a sled in the snow.

A Siberian husky has large flat feet that help it run on soft snow without sinking.

Siberian huskies have two thick coats of fur to protect them in temperatures as low as -75°F (-59°C).

Siberian huskies also work well in groups. When they are as young as two months old, husky puppies can be **hitched** to a sled and taught basic **commands**. Together, they learn when to run, stop, and turn in different directions, as well as to stay focused on pulling the sled. These **traits** allow the dogs to work together as a strong team.

**These Siberian husky puppies rest after a day of training.**

# Underdog

Leonhard Seppala, the fastest musher in Alaska, **volunteered** to drive one of the sled teams. He raced to his **kennel** to build a team of his twenty best huskies. Togo, his trusted lead dog, would go up front as always.

Leonhard and Togo were famous throughout Alaska for their speed in sled races.

A lead dog works with a musher to guide the rest of the team. Dogs that have great intelligence, speed, and courage are chosen as lead dogs.

There was a young black husky that did not get chosen. His name was Balto. Leonhard felt that Balto didn't have enough experience to join the team. In addition, he wasn't as fast or as strong as the other dogs. Leonhard and his sled team left for their position on the trail for the relay. Soon enough, however, Balto would get his chance to prove Leonhard wrong.

Leonhard thought Balto, shown here, was not ready for such a long run.

# Racing Against Time

A train brought the medicine from Anchorage as far north as Nenana, Alaska, where the railroad tracks met the sled trail to Nome. From there, it was up to the dogsled teams to travel the remaining 674 miles (1,085 km). It was January 27, and "Wild Bill" Shannon and his lead dog, Blackie, were up first. As soon as the train arrived, Wild Bill grabbed the antitoxin and raced off for Tolovana, where the next team was waiting.

"Wild Bill" grabbed the medicine from a train like this one and raced toward Nome with his team of dogs.

All together, the teams of sled dogs would run nearly 700 miles (1,127 km) through Alaska.

Nome

Bluff

**ALASKA**

Norton Sound

train route

Nenana

Pacific Ocean

Anchorage

As the dog teams **braved** -50°F (-46°C) weather, there was more bad news from Nome. The disease was spreading fast. More volunteers were needed to take part in the relay to help get the antitoxin to Nome more quickly. Gunnar Kaasen, Leonhard's assistant, asked to help. He raced to the kennel, grabbed his favorite husky, and placed him at the front of the sled. Balto now had his chance to be a lead dog.

Gunnar Kaasen is sitting with his team of sled dogs. Balto is standing on the top row, second from left.

It was so cold on the trail that one musher's hand froze to his sled. Steaming hot water was needed to pry it loose.

# Crossing Norton Sound

For four days, the first dog teams raced toward Nome. The most dangerous part of the trail—the Norton Sound—was still ahead. The Norton Sound is an **inlet** covered mostly by ice. Because of strong winds, however, some of the ice can break off and float into the sea. As a result, a dog team crossing the Sound can drown or **drift** off to sea in seconds—and be lost forever.

The Norton Sound

To be safe, most mushers chose to go around the Norton Sound—even though it took more time. However, Leonhard Seppala didn't want to waste any time. With the children's lives at stake, Leonhard trusted Togo to safely bring him across the sound. Togo didn't disappoint him.

Leonhard and his trusted lead dog, Togo, began their leg of the race on January 31.

During the race to Nome, Leonhard and Togo traveled a greater distance than any other dogsled team.

17

# Balto Takes the Lead

On February 1, Gunnar and Balto were ready for their turn in the relay. They waited in a small cabin in Bluff, Alaska, about 50 miles (81 km) from Nome. Balto snacked on dried salmon, as Gunnar watched for the next musher to appear. Charlie Olson and his lead dog, Jack, had picked up the antitoxin from Leonhard earlier in the day. At 7:00 P.M., a shout could be heard outside. The medicine had arrived!

Cabins, like this one, offered a place for mushers and their dogs to stay warm while waiting for their turn in the relay.

Charlie stumbled into the cabin. He couldn't move his fingers due to **frostbite**. His dogs were nearly frozen. A blizzard had hit the trail. Charlie warned Gunnar to wait for better weather. Gunnar, however, wouldn't be stopped. Balto and Gunnar were the second-to-last dog team, and Nome's children were waiting. With a shout, Gunnar commanded Balto to lead the other dogs into the blizzard.

Frostbitten fingers often fill with blood and turn black.

Many sled dogs refuse to run during a blizzard. However, Balto (shown here with Gunnar) bravely led his team during the blinding snowstorm.

After Gunnar and Balto's team left the cabin, Nome's mayor sent a **telegram** telling the last two mushers to wait for better weather. Gunnar would never get that message.

# Lost Trail

A few hours after leaving the cabin, Gunnar and Balto hit their first **obstacle**: a huge **snowdrift** that blocked the trail. Gunnar had no choice but to leave the trail. He hoped that Balto would find the path again, but it was pitch black outside. Balto sniffed the snow, trying to find the scent of the trail. Suddenly, Balto lifted his head, barked, and broke into a run. He had found it!

A dogsled team races across the snow.

A Siberian husky's sense of smell is 600 to 700 times better than a human's.

Unfortunately, the danger didn't end there. A few miles later, the team had to cross the frozen Topkok River. At the river's edge, Balto stopped in his tracks and wouldn't move forward. Gunnar heard his lead dog's message loud and clear: The ice was too weak to cross. Gunnar immediately led the team away from the river to safer ground.

**A sled dog team near the Topkok River**

# Almost Disaster

During the night, Balto carefully led his team around the Topkok River and then over the Topkok Mountains. **Ferocious** winds swirled the snow in the air. Gunnar could hardly see the dogs in front of the sled. A huge blast of wind pounded the sled, flipped it on its side, and dumped it into a **snowbank**.

**A dogsled team on top of the Topkok Mountains in Alaska**

To flip a fully loaded sled, winds must blow as fast as 60 to 70 miles per hour (97 to 113 kph)—or as fast as a car speeding down a highway.

Gunnar reached into the sled to find the medicine. It was gone! If he couldn't find it, the children would die. Gunnar threw off his gloves and desperately dug his hands into the snow. Finally, he hit something hard. It was the antitoxin! Relieved, Gunnar fixed the sled and directed Balto toward the town of Port Safety, where the last musher was supposed to be waiting.

A dogsled similar to the one used by Gunnar and Balto

# Arrival in Nome

When the sled arrived at Port Safety, Gunnar noticed something odd. The lights of the cabin were off. The last musher had gotten the mayor's message to wait out the storm and had gone to sleep. Gunnar could wake him, but they were only 20 miles (32 km) away from Nome. Gunnar knew that Balto and his team could make it the rest of the way.

The people of Nome excitedly waited for Balto and Gunnar to arrive with the antitoxin.

On the morning of February 2, Balto and his team finally arrived in Nome. Gunnar stumbled off the sled, petted his beloved Balto, and then passed out from **exhaustion**. The previous record for a sled trip from Nenana to Nome had been nine days. The heroic sled dog teams had made the trip in five and a half days!

By the time the medicine reached Nome, it was frozen solid even though it had been wrapped in blankets. The medicine was put in a warm room to thaw before it could be used.

Balto and his teammates in Nome after delivering the antitoxin

# A National Hero

Dr. Welch gave the medicine to the sick children, which saved their lives. Within two weeks, Nome had returned to normal. Life, however, would never be the same for Balto. Children throughout the country wrote him fan letters. In New York City, a statue was created in his honor. Balto had come a long way from not making Leonhard's team!

Balto's statue in New York City's Central Park

President Calvin Coolidge awarded each musher a gold medal.

Even though sled dogs are no longer used for transportation in Alaska, they are still used for sport. The Iditarod Race, which follows part of the trail used by the relay dogs, is the most popular sporting event in the state. The race still remembers the heroes of 1925. At the 2005 race, 81-year-old Jirdes Winther Baxter was made an **honorary** musher. When she was just a year old, she was saved by the medicine brought by Balto and his heroic **canine** teammates.

A team racing during the Iditarod

Jirdes Winther Baxter, mother of six, survived diphtheria due to the hard work of Balto and the other dogs.

# Just the Facts

- The coldest temperature ever recorded in Alaska is -80°F (-62°C).

- One of the greatest natural threats to dog teams in Alaska is a charging moose, which can weigh up to 1,500 pounds (680 kg). When hungry, a moose may try to kick or stamp on dogs to reach food stored on a sled.

- In the last ten years, there has not been a recorded case of diphtheria in the United States.

- After Balto stopped working as a sled dog, he spent the end of his life in Cleveland, Ohio. After he died, the city's natural history museum stuffed Balto, preserving him so that future generations could see the heroic dog.

Siberian huskies, as well as other breeds, are used as sled dogs:

Siberian husky

Greenland dog

Alaskan husky

Malamute

**antitoxin** (*an*-ti-*TOKS*-in) a medicine used to fight a specific poison or bacteria

**blizzard** (BLIZ-urd) snow combined with high winds and low visibility

**braved** (BRAYVD) faced without showing fear

**bred** (BRED) when dogs from specific breeds are mated to produce puppies with certain characteristics

**canine** (KAY-nine) an animal that is a member of the dog family

**commands** (kuh-MANDS) orders given by someone to do certain things

**contagious** (kuhn-TAY-juhss) able to be passed from person to person

**diphtheria** (dip-THEER-ee-uh) a deadly disease that occurs in the nose and throat

**disease** (duh-ZEEZ) sickness or illness

**drift** (DRIFT) to be carried along by water or wind

**epidemic** (*ep*-uh-DEM-ik) a disease that spreads quickly

**exhaustion** (eg-ZAWST-chuhn) a state of extreme tiredness

**ferocious** (fuh-ROH-shuhss) fierce

**frostbite** (FRAWST-*bite*) the freezing of skin due to extreme cold

**hitched** (HICHT) fastened to something with a rope or other item

**honorary** (AH-nuh-*rare*-ee) given as an honor without the usual requirements or duties

**inlet** (IN-let) a narrow body of water running from a larger body of water, such as an ocean, onto land

**kennel** (KEN-uhl) a place where dogs are raised or trained

**lead dog** (LEED DAWG) a dog that heads a team of sled dogs

**musher** (MUSH-ur) the driver of a dogsled

**obstacle** (OB-stuh-kuhl) a thing that blocks a path

**relay** (REE-lay) passing an object from one team to another; it allows a race to move faster because it replaces tired racers with new ones

**snowbank** (SNOH-bank) a large mound of snow

**snowdrift** (SNOH-*drift*) a pile of snow created by the wind

**telegram** (TEL-uh-gram) a message sent by a special device over long distances

**traits** (TRAYTS) qualities or characteristics

**vaccine** (vak-SEEN) medicine that protects people from a disease

**volunteered** (*vol*-uhn-TIHRD) offered to do a job without pay

## Bibliography

**Houdek, Jennifer, and Tricia Brown.** "Togo and Balto, Dog Heroes." *University of Alaska, Anchorage, Lit Site.* (www.litsite.org/index.cfm?section=Digital-Archives&page=Land-Sea-Air&cat=Dog-Mushing&viewpost=2&ContentId=2561)

**Houdek, Jennifer.** "The Serum Race of 1925." *University of Alaska, Anchorage, Lit Site.* (www.litsite.org/index.cfm?section=Digital-Archives&page=Land-Sea-Air&cat=Dog-Mushing&viewpost=2&ContentId=2559)

**Salisbury, Gay, and Laney Salisbury.** *The Cruelest Miles: The Heroic Story of Dogs and Men in a Race Against an Epidemic.* New York: W.W. Norton & Co. (2003).

## Read More

**Funk, Joe.** *Mush! Sled Dogs of the Iditarod.* New York: Scholastic (2013).

**Kimmel, Elizabeth Cody.** *Balto and the Great Race.* New York: Random House (1999).

**Miller, Debbie S.** *The Great Serum Race: Blazing the Iditarod Trail.* New York: Walker Children's (2006).

**Person, Stephen.** *Sled Dog: Powerful Miracle (Built for Cold: Arctic Animals).* New York: Bearport (2011).

## Learn More Online

Visit these Web sites to learn more about Balto, Siberian huskies, and other sled dogs:

**www.akc.org/breeds/siberian_husky/index.cfm**

**www.cmnh.org/visit/exhibits/balto**

**www.iditarod.com**

**www.pbs.org/wnet/nature/episodes/sled-dogs-an-alaskan-epic/introduction/3146/**

## About the Author

Kevin Blake lives in Portland, Oregon, with his wife, Melissa, and his son, Sam. He dedicates this book to both of them.